Robert Burns, Alexander Leighton

The Principal Songs of Robert Burns

Translated into Mediaeval Latin Verse, with the Scottish Version Collated

Robert Burns, Alexander Leighton

The Principal Songs of Robert Burns
Translated into Mediaeval Latin Verse, with the Scottish Version Collated

ISBN/EAN: 9783744661829

Printed in Europe, USA, Canada, Australia, Japan

Cover: Foto ©Thomas Meinert / pixelio.de

More available books at **www.hansebooks.com**

THE PRINCIPAL

SONGS OF ROBERT BURNS

TRANSLATED INTO MEDIÆVAL LATIN VERSE,

WITH THE

SCOTTISH VERSION COLLATED.

BY

ALEXANDER LEIGHTON,

AUTHOR OF " CURIOUS STORIED TRADITIONS OF SCOTTISH LIFE,"
" THE COURT OF CACUS," ETC.

EDINBURGH:
WILLIAM P. NIMMO, ST DAVID STREET.
LONDON: HOULSTON & WRIGHT, PATERNOSTER ROW.

MDCCCLXII.

PREFACE.

In offering this *jeu d'esprit* to the public, the author has been
influenced by one or two considerations. In the first place, translations of this kind have heretofore been proved acceptable to a
class including many who are only partially acquainted with the
Latin tongue—a thorough knowledge of which is really not required for comprehending and enjoying—in so far as it is capable
of yielding enjoyment—this species of literature. And certainly
there is no reason, so long as translations of works of fancy into
modern tongues are found readable and pleasant, why Latin, the
most generally known of all the dead languages, should be ex-
cluded. It may more generally be argued, that as we are by
nature pleased with changes of dress, varieties in colour, and altera-
tions of form in material objects, so we may feel satisfaction in seeing
ingenious ideas and beautiful sentiments in a new garb. In the
second place, I have long been of opinion, that as the *paterfamilias*
in the *Gentleman's Magazine* proposed to allure his sons to Latin

through the mean of a translation of Lullabolero, or some other of the popular songs they were in the habit of either singing or whistling, so one might, through the translated medium of such charming lyrics as those of Burns—especially when already committed to the memory—find a mode of removing that disinclination which is often so great a barrier to the attainment of the language. The school might take a lesson from the nursery : the youngsters will accept the bitter powder concealed in sweets; and we all know, as regards adults, how much there is of allurement concealed behind the ostensible motive, even in what we proudly call the duties of life, not excepting considerable self-sacrifices. In the third place, there can be no objection on the part of the admirers of Burns—and we could hope these were all mankind—to see a small tribute of this kind offered to his genius, whereby those lyrics, which speak to all hearts, may be attainable by many who, ignorant of Scotch and English, enjoy the possession of what is yet, in a sense, the most general, as it is the most beautiful of all languages.

Even if these reasons did not justify my whim, it is scarcely worth the pains to corrugate the brows over what was intended to relax and enliven them.

As for the severe scholars, who are so jealous of an encroachment on the confines of the purely classic, I may perhaps conciliate them by the admission that I make no pretensions to classical Latinity; and to the answer, that it was not for one with such a confession in his mouth to attempt so critical an undertaking, the reply may be permitted—that while mere grammatical accuracy is not the only qualification needed, there is required in the peculiar case of rendering from a tongue which is that of the people to whom the rendering is addressed, so much of accommodation to the idioms of the home language as to be incompatible with a very strict adherence to those of the foreign.

Finally, where the work must, by its nature, be so far prolusive, there are liberties and means—not always very legitimate—of getting over difficulties which the generous scholar is never slow to acknowledge and forgive.

York Lodge, Trinity,
December 1861.

CONTENTS.

Decies repetita placebit.

Highland Mary.

——

THE banks and braes, and streams around
        The Castle o' Montgomery,
Green be your woods, and fair your flow'rs,
        Your waters never drumlie.
There simmer first unfaulds her robes,
        And there they langest tarry :
For there I took the last fareweel
        Of my dear Highland Mary.

How sweetly bloom'd the gay green birk,
        How rich the hawthorn's blossom,
As underneath their fragrant shade
        I clasp'd her to my bosom ;
The golden hours, on angel wings,
        Flew o'er me and my dearie ;
For dear to me as light and life
        Was my sweet Highland Mary.

Wi' mony a vow, and lock'd embrace,
        Our parting was fu' tender,
And pledging aft to meet again,
        We tore ourselves asunder.

Ribi flubii circiter.

———

RIVI fluvii circiter
    Castellum Montis Gomeri,
Sylvæ montes floresque,
    Aquæ nunquam turbidæ.
Evolvat vestes ibi ver,
    Cunctetur et longissime,
Nam ibi dixi valeas !
    Caræ meæ Mariæ.

Quam odorata betula !
    Quam comptæ flores spinæ !
Dum sub eorum umbra
    Compressi illam pectori.
Horæ fugerunt aureæ
    Sciente me nec cara mi,
Nam cara mi ut lumen est
    Dulcis erat Maria.

Cum votis et amplexibus
    Nos separamur tenerè,
Et convenire iterum
    Voventes nos abiimus ;

But oh ! fell death's untimely frost,
  That nipt my flow'r so early ;
Now green's the sod, and cauld's the clay,
  That wraps my Highland Mary.

O pale, pale now, those rosy lips,
  I aft hae kissed so fondly !
And clos'd for aye the sparkling glance
  That dwelt on me sae kindly !
And mouldering now, in silent dust,
  That heart that lo'ed me dearly ;
But still within my bosom's core
  Shall live my Highland Mary.

Heu ! mortis gelu subito
  Avulsit meum florem,
Et cespites et lutum nunc
  Involvunt meam Mariam.

Nunc pallida hæc labia
  Quæ osculare sueveram,
Occlusi sunt hi oculi
  Qui placidè mi riserant.
Resolvitur in pulverem
  Cor quod amavit intimè ;
Sed semper meo pectore
  Manebit mea Maria.

I am a son of Mars.

I AM a son of Mars, who have been in many wars,
  And show my cuts and scars wherever I come ;
This here was for a wench, and that other in a trench,
  When welcoming the French at the sound of the drum.

My prentiship I past where my leader breath'd his last,
  When the bloody die was cast on the heights of Abram ;
I serv'd out my trade when the gallant game was play'd,
  And the Moro low was laid at the sound of the drum.

I lastly was with Curtis, among the floating batt'ries,
  And there I left for witnesses an arm and a limb ;
Yet let my country need me, with Elliott to head me,
  I'd clatter on my stumps at the sound of the drum.

And now, tho' I must beg, with a wooden arm and leg,
  And many a tatter'd rag hanging over my bum,
I'm as happy with my wallet, my bottle, and my callet,
  As when I us'd in scarlet to follow the drum.

What tho' with hoary locks, I must stand the windy shocks,
  Beneath the woods and rocks, oftentimes for a home ;
When the tother bag I sell, and the tother bottle tell,
  I could meet a troop of hell at the sound of the drum.

Engalii filius in multis fui proeliis.

——

NYALII filius in multis fui proeliis,
    Ostendo mea vulnera quocunque veniam
Hoc fero pro ancilla, et illud ex fossula,
    Cum Gallos gratularer—ad tonans tympanum.

Duxi tirocinium cum ductor meus obiit
    Et jactæ essent aleæ per colles de Abram,
Ejus agmina sequebar cum ludus luderetur
    Et Moro sterneretur—ad tonans tympanum.

Ultimo cum Curti, inter nantia pugnacula,
    Reliqui qua pro testibus et crus et brachium ;
Si oporteat armare, et sub Elliot pugnare,
    Super truncos strepitabo—ad tonans tympanum.

Licet me mendicare cum tibia lignari',
    Pendentibus panniculis super dorsum ;
Beatus crumenella et utre et puella,
    Ut solet in coccineo sectari tympanum.

Etiamsi sit mi ferre procellas super terra
    Per scopulos et sylvulas tanquam domum ;
Cum vendam meum sacculum et alterum utriculum,
    Diabolis obstarem—ad tonans tympanum.

The Lea Rig.

WHEN o'er the hill the eastern star
  Tells bughtin-time is near, my jo ;
And owsen frae the furrow'd field
  Return sae dowf and weary O ;
Down by the burn, where scented birks
  Wi' dew are hanging clear, my jo,
I'll meet thee on the lea rig,
  My ain kind dearie O.

In mirkest glen, at midnight hour,
  I'd rove, and ne'er be eerie O,
If thro' that glen I gaed to thee,
  My ain kind dearie O.
Altho' the night were ne'er sae wild,
  And I were ne'er sae wearie O,
I'd meet thee on the lea rig,
  My ain kind dearie O.

The hunter lo'es the morning sun,
  To rouse the mountain deer, my jo ;
At noon the fisher seeks the glen,
  Along the burn to steer, my jo ;

Cum stella vespertina.

—

CUM stella vespertina
  Dat oves ad ovile O ;
Et boves ex agello,
  Incipiunt redire O,
Per ripas ubi betulæ
  Impendent rorulentæ O,
Conveniam super liras
  Me' ipsius caram O.

Obscuro loco noctu,
  Vagarer sine metu O,
Pervenerim si apud te,
  Me' ipsius caram O.
Licet nox ferissima,
  Et ego lassus nihil-O,
Adirem te per liras,
  Me' ipsius cara O.

Venator amat solem,
  Cervarum citatorem O,
Piscator quærit sylvas,
  Per ripas indagare O.

Gi'e me the hour o' gloaming grey,
It maks my heart sae cheery O,
To meet thee on the lea rig,
My ain kind dearie O.

Da mihi horam vesperam
Exhilarat mi pectus O,
Ad liras convenire
Meam solam caram O.

My Nannie, O.

BEHIND yon hills, where Lugar flows,
　　Mang moors and mosses many, O,
The wintry sun the day has clos'd,
　　And I'll awa to Nannie, O.
The westlin' wind blaws loud an' shrill ;
　　The night's baith mirk an' rainy, O ;
But I'll get my plaid, an' out I'll steal,
　　An' owre the hills to Nannie, O.

My Nannie's charming, sweet, an' young :
　　Nae artfu' wiles to win ye, O :
May ill befa' the flattering tongue
　　That wad beguile my Nannie, O.
Her face is fair, her heart is true,
　　She's spotless as she's bonnie, O :
The op'ning gowan, wet wi' dew,
　　Nae purer is than Nannie, O.

A country lad is my degree,
　　And few there be that ken me, O ;
But what care I how few they be ?
　　I'm welcome aye to Nannie, O.

Post colles ubi interfluit.

POST colles ubi interfluit,
    Lugar paludes multas, O,
Brumalis sol fert vesperum,
    Et ibo ad me' Annam, O.
Canorus ventus perstrepit,
    Nox ater pluvialis, O,
Mi sumam meum gausape,
    Et ibo ad me' Annam, O.

Me' Anna pulchra juvenis,
    In illa nullus dolus, O ;
Infelix ille ! lingua qui
    Deciperet me' Annam, O.
Facies suavis, verum cor,
    Quam pura ac est bella, O ;
Dispandens rosa roscida,
    Non pulchrior est quam Anna, O.

Sum puer pauper rusticus,
    Et pauci noscitant me, O ;
Quid mea refert quam pauci,
    Si gratus apud Annam, O.

My riches a' 's my penny-fee,
  An' I maun guide it cannie, O ;
But warl's gear ne'er troubles me,
  My thoughts are a' my Nannie, O.

Our auld guidman delights to view
  His sheep an' kye thrive bonnie, O ;
But I'm as blythe that hauds his pleugh,
  An' has nae care but Nannie, O.
Come weel, come woe, I care na by,
  I'll tak' what Heav'n will sen' me, O ;
Nae ither care in life have I,
  But live, an' love my Nannie, O.

Mercos denarii res me' est,
  Oportet sim perparcus, O ;
Mundanæ res non angunt me,
  Me' cura est me' Anna, O.

Seni nostro libeat
  Videre oves multas, O ;
Beatior Ego qui aro,
  Nil cura nisi Anna, O.
Adsit bonum adsit malum,
  Accipi' quæ dant cœli, O ;
In vita nulla cura mi,
  Ni vivere cum Anna, O.

The Winsome Wee Thing.

SHE is a winsome wee thing,
She is a handsome wee thing,
She is a bonnie wee thing,
This sweet wee wife o' mine.

I never saw a fairer,
I never lo'ed a dearer,
And niest my heart I'll wear her,
For fear my jewel tine.
        She is, etc.

The warld's wrack we share o't,
The warstle and the care o't,
Wi' her I'll blythely bear it,
And think my lot divine.
        She is, etc.

Me' uxor est tenella.

Me' uxor est tenella,
Me' uxor est pulchella,
Me' uxor una bella,
Hæc uxor tenuis mi.

Non videris pulchriorem,
Non videris cariorem,
Focillo me' uxorem,
Ne illam perderem.
                Me' uxor, etc.

Mala participamus,
Et curas toleramus,
Invicem nos amamus,
Beatusque credam.
                Me' uxor, etc.

Duncan Gray.

DUNCAN Gray cam' here to woo,
　Ha! ha! the wooing o't!
On blithe yule night when we were fou,
　Ha! ha! the wooing o't!
Maggie coost her head fu' high,
Look'd asklent and unco skeigh,
Gart poor Duncan stand abeigh ;
　Ha! ha! the wooing o't!

Duncan fleech'd, and Duncan pray'd,
　Ha! ha! the wooing o't!
Meg was deaf as Ailsa Craig,
　Ha! ha! the wooing o't!
Duncan sigh'd baith out and in,
Grat his een baith bleert and blin',
Spak' o' lowpin' o'er a linn ;
　Ha! ha! the wooing o't!

Time and chance are but a tide,
　Ha! ha! the wooing o't!
Slighted love is sair to bide,
　Ha! ha! the wooing o't!

Duncanus Canus venit nobis.

—

UNCANUS Canus venit nobis,
  Ha! ha! amores hi!
Festu quum inebriabamus,
  Ha! ha! amores hi!
Caput Maggea jactabat,
Oculos et obliquabat,
Duncanum fastu pertractabat,
  Ha! ha! amores hi!

Duncanus videns et orabat,
  Ha! ha! amores hi!
Maggea surdula fiebat,
  Ha! ha! amores hi!
Duncanus miser suspirabat,
In cæcitatem lacrymabat,
Et moriturum prædicabat,
  Ha! ha! amores hi!

Fluit tempus, fluit casus,
  Ha! ha! amores hi!
Æstuat contemptus amor,
  Ha! ha! amores hi!

Shall I, like a fool, quoth he,
For a haughty lizzie die?
She may gae to—France for me!
Ha! ha! the wooing o't!

How it comes let doctors tell,
Ha! ha! the wooing o't!
Meg grew sick—as he grew hale,
Ha! ha! the wooing o't!
Something in her bosom wrings,
For relief a sigh she brings;
And O, her een, they spak' sic things!
Ha! ha! the wooing o't!

Duncan was a lad o' grace,
Ha! ha! the wooing o't!
Maggie's was a piteous case,
Ha! ha! the wooing o't!
Duncan couldna be her death,
Swelling pity smoor'd his wrath;
Now they're crouse and canty baith,
Ha! ha! the wooing o't!

" Moriar ?" dicit sibi,
" Partem ludens fatui
" Galliam abeat—pro me !"
  Ha ! ha ! amores hi !

Qua evenit—dum valebat,
  Ha ! ha ! amores hi !
Maggea sequens ægrotabat,
  Ha ! ha ! amores hi !
Aliquid in corde radit,
Lenis gemitus evadit,
Lacryma per genas cadit,
  Ha ! ha ! amores hi !

Duncanus vir est lepidus,
  Ha ! ha ! amores hi !
Maggeæ erant male res,
  Ha ! ha ! amores hi !
Ille non occideret,
Ejus illum miseret,
Nuptias quisque dixerit,
  Ha ! ha ! amores hi !

Green Grow the Rashes.

GREEN grow the rashes, O!
Green grow the rashes, O!
The sweetest hours that e'er I spend,
Are spent amang the lasses, O.

There's nought but care on ev'ry han',
In ev'ry hour that passes, O:
What signifies the life o' man,
An' twere na for the lasses, O?
Green grows, etc.

The war'ly race may riches chase,
An' riches still may fly them, O;
And tho' at last they catch them fast,
Their hearts can ne'er enjoy them, O.
Green grows, etc.

But gi'e me a canny hour at e'en,
My arms about my dearie, O;
An' war'ly cares, and war'ly men,
May a' gae tapsalteerie, O!
Green grows, etc.

Crescant juncilli, O.

———

CRESCANT juncilli, O ;
　Crescant juncilli, O ;
Nulla vita dulcior
　Quam vita cum puellis, O.

Est nil ni cura undique,
　In unaquaque hora, O :
Quid pretii ! vita hominis
　Absente dulci corcul-O.
　　Crescant, etc.

Avari rem venati sint,
　Divitiæ effugiunt, O ;
Et forte si arreptæ sint,
　Corda non delectant, O.
　　Crescant, etc.

Da mihi horam vesperam,
　Cum meo desideri-O ;
Mundanæ curæ, homines,
　Vadant in tapsaltcerie, O.
　　Crescant, etc.

For you sae douse, ye sneer at this,
    Ye're nought but senseless asses, O ;
The wisest man the warl' e'er saw,
    He dearly lov'd the lasses, O.
        Green grows, etc.

Auld Nature swears, the lovely dears,
    Her noblest work she classes, O :
Her 'prentice han' she tried on man,
    An' then she made the lasses, O.
        Green grows, etc.

Prudentes irridētis vos,
Exanimi aselli ! O ;
Salomo sapientior
Has amavit belle ! O.
    Crescant, etc.

Natura jurat " femina !
Supremo anticellis, O !"
Tironis manus hominem
Formavit tunc puellas, O.
    Crescant, etc.

The Rigs o' Barley.

IT was upon a Lammas night,
    When corn rigs are bonnie,
Beneath the moon's unclouded light,
    I held away to Annie :
The time flew by wi' tentless heed,
    Till 'tween the late and early,
Wi' sma' persuasion she agreed
    To see me thro' the barley.

The sky was blue, the wind was still,
    The moon was shining clearly :
I set her down, wi' right good will,
    Amang the rigs o' barley.
I kent her heart was a' my ain :
    I lov'd her most sincerely ;
I kiss'd her owre and owre again,
    Amang the rigs o' barley.

I lock'd her in my fond embrace !
    Her heart was beating rarely :
My blessings on that happy place,
    Amang the rigs o' barley.

Clara nocte sextili.

CLARA nocte sextili,
  Quum segetes sunt fulgidæ,
Sub lunæ claro lumine
  Ad Annam festinavi.
Fugit tempus furtivè,
  Usq' ad noctem mediam ;
Annuit me comitem
  Ducere per hordeum.

Sub æthere ceruleo,
  Lucente luna lucidè ;
Illam sponte posui
  Inter liras hordei.
Cor ejus novi totum mi,
  Amavi illam fervidè ;
Multa dedi oscula
  Inter liras hordei.

Amplexus sum in brachiis,
  Cor palpitat acerrimè ;
Id loci cœlis gratum sit
  Inter liras hordei.

But by the moon and stars so bright,
　　That shone that hour so clearly !
She aye shall bless that happy night,
　　Amang the rigs o' barley.

I ha'e been blithe wi' comrades dear ;
　　I ha'e been merry drinking ;
I ha'e been joyfu' gatherin' gear,
　　I ha'e been happy thinkin' :
But a' the pleasures e'er I saw,
　　Tho' three times doubled fairly,
That happy night was worth them a',
　　Amang the rigs o' barley.

Nam per stellas lunamque,
  Quæ luxit adeo lucidè,
Beabit illa loculum
  Inter liras hordei.

Lætatus sum cum amicis,
  Lætatus sum cum convivis,
Lætatus sum lucrando,
  Lætatus cogitando.
Sed quantacunque illa sint
  Tripliciter notata,
Instar omnium illa nox
  Inter liras hordei.

Thou hast left me ever, Jamie.

THOU hast left me ever, Jamie!
　　Thou hast left me ever;
Thou hast left me ever, Jamie;
　　Thou hast left me ever.
Aften hast thou vow'd that death
　　Only should us sever;
Now thou'st left thy lass for aye,—
　　I maun see thee never, Jamie,
　　I'll see thee never.

Thou hast me forsaken, Jamie!
　　Thou hast me forsaken;
Thou hast me forsaken, Jamie!
　　Thou hast me forsaken.
Thou canst love anither jo,
　　While my heart is breaking;
Soon my weary een I'll close—
　　Never mair to waken, Jamie,
　　Never mair to waken.

Reliquisti me, Jacobe.

ELIQUISTI me, Jacobe!
Me revises nunquam,
Reliquisti me, Jacobe!
Revises me, oh! nunquam.
Jurasti sæpe tu mortem
Nos separaturam tantum,
Caram reliquisti tu,
Te videbo nunquam,
Videbo te, oh! nunquam.

Deseruisti me, Jacobe!
Me revises nunquam,
Deseruisti me, Jacobe!
Revises me, oh! nunquam.
Ames caram alteram
Me moriento sensim,
Occludam oculos meos,
Heu! solvendos nunquam,
Heu! solvendos nunquam

39

The Posie.

O LUVE will venture in,
  Where it daurna weel be seen,
O luve will venture in,
  Where wisdom ance has been ;
But I will down yon river rove,
  Amang the woods sae green,—
And a' to pu' a posie
  To my ain dear May.

The primrose I will pu',
  The firstling o' the year,
And I will pu' the pink,
  The emblem o' my dear ;
For she's the pink o' womankind,
  And blooms without a peer ;
And a' to be a posie
  To my ain dear May.

I'll pu' the budding rose,
  When Phœbus peeps in view,
For it's like a baumy kiss
  O' her sweet bonnie mou' ;

Oh! intrabit amor.

OH! intrabit amor
  Qua ægre audeat,
Oh! intrabit amor
  Qua sapientia stat;
Sed vadam inter sylvulas
  Per rivulos atque.
Nam ego carpam corrolam
  Me' care Maiæ.

Primulam Ego carpam
  Primitias anni,
Et etiam caryophyllum
  Signum care me'.
Nam illa flos femineæ
  Ac floret diutinè.
Et omnes nectent coroliam
  Me' caræ Maiæ.

Rosam carpam teneram
  Dispandentem se,
Et suaviolo similem
  Oris me' mellullæ,

41

The hyacinth's for constancy,
   Wi' its unchanging blue,—
And a' to be a posie
   To my ain dear May.

The lily it is pure,
   And the lily it is fair,
And in her lovely bosom
   I'll place the lily there ;
The daisy's for simplicity,
   And unaffected air,—
And a' to be a posie
   To my ain dear May.

The hawthorn I will pu',
   Wi' its locks o' siller gray,
Where, like an aged man,
   It stands at break o' day.
But the songster's nest within the bush
   I winna take away,—
And a' to be a posie
   To my ain dear May.

The woodbine I will pu',
   When the e'ening star is near,
And the diamond-draps o' dew
   Shall be her een sae clear :
The violet's for modesty,
   Which weel she fa's to wear,—
And a' to be a posie
   To my ain dear May.

Et florem hyacynthanum
  Constantem verumque.
Hi omnes nectent corollam
  Me' caræ Maiæ.

Lilium est purum,
  Formosum lilium,
Et pectore in ejus
  Apponam lilium,
Bellis est suavissima,
  Simplex et facio.
Omnes hi nectent corrollam
  Me' caræ Maiæ.

Et florem spinæ carpam
  Coma argentea,
Qui sicut homo senex
  Stat luce dubia.
Sed nidulam, avicula!
  Non rapiam a te.
Omnes hi nectent corollam
  Me' caræ Maiæ.

Et caprifolium carpam
  Cum vesper presto sit,
Et omnis stilla roris
  Ejus oculus erit,
Violam pro modestia
  Quam decet gerere.
Omnes hi nectent corollam
  Me' caræ Maiæ.

I'll tie the posie round
  Wi' the silken band o' luve,
And I'll place it in her breast,
  And I'll swear by a' above,
That to my latest draught o' life
  The band shall ne'er remuve,—
And this will be a posie
  To my ain dear May.

Corollam tunc prætexam
 Vitta cum serica ;
In gremio atque ponam
 Vovebo et—" illa
Ad vitam perlongissimam
 Non unquam solvenda."
Omnes hi nectent corollam
 Me' caræ Maiæ.

To Mary in Heaven.

THOU lingering star, with less'ning ray,
    That lov'st to greet the early morn,
Again thou usher'st in the day
    My Mary from my soul was torn.
O Mary! dear departed shade!
    Where is thy place of blissful rest?
See'st thou thy lover lowly laid?
    Hear'st thou the groans that rend his breast ?

That sacred hour can I forget,
    Can I forget the hallowed grove,
Where by the winding Ayr we met,
    To live one day of parting love !
Eternity will not efface,
    Those records dear of transports past ;
Thy image at our last embrace ;
    Ah! little thought we 'twas our last!

Ayr gurgling kissed his pebbled shore,
    O'erhung with wild woods, thick'ning, green ;
The fragrant birch, and hawthorn hoar,
    Twin'd amorous round the raptured scene.

Tu stella tarda cujus radius.

U stellâ tarda cujus radius,
  Salutem indicat Auroræ,
Iterum introducis diem
  Quo mea obiit María.
Oh Mari'! umbra lapsa cara!
  Ubi beatæ locus pacis?
An vides amatorem tuum?
  An audis ejus gemitus?

An sanctæ horæ obliviscar,
  An obliviscar sylvulæ
Ad rivum ubi convenimus,
  Amoris diem ducere!
Nunquam æternitas delebit
  Vestigia hæc impetuum
Quàm minimum heu! censui
  Amplexum illum ultimum.

Ayr strepens osculavit ripas,
  Pendente dum sub sylyula,
Et spinula et betula
  Ramos intertexuerunt.

The flowers sprang wanton to be prest,
    The birds sang love on every spray,
'Till too, too soon, the glowing west,
    Proclaimed the speed of winged day.

Still o'er these scenes my mem'ry wakes,
    And fondly broods with miser care ;
Time but the impression stronger makes,
    As streams their channels deeper wear.
My Mary, dear departed shade !
    Where is thy place of blissful rest ?
See'st thou thy lover lowly laid ?
Hear'st thou the groans that rend his breast ?

Flores compremi exsultant,
　Cantillant aves lepidè,
Donec cito nimium sol
　Dedit locum vesperi.

Has scenas supervigilo,
　Et curæ incubo meæ:
Vestigia tempus excăvat
　Æque ac ripas rivuli.
Oh Mari'! umbra lapsa cara!
　Ubi beatæ locus pacis?
An vides amatorem tuum?
　An audis ejus gemitus?

49　　　　　ᴵᴵ

Willie Brew'd a Peck o' Maut.

WILLIE brew'd a peck o' maut,
And Rob and Allan cam' to pree;
Three blither hearts that lee-lang night,
Ye wad na find in Christendie.
    We are na fou, we're no that fou,
    But just a drappie in our e'e;
    The cock may craw, the day may daw,
    An' aye we'll taste the barley bree.

Here are we met, three merry boys,
Three merry boys I trow are we;
And mony a night we've merry been,
And mony mae we hope to be!
    We are na fou, etc.

It is the moon, I ken her horn,
That's blinking in the lift sae hie;
She shines sae bright to wyle us hame,
But by my sooth she'll wait a wee!
    We are na fou, etc.

—

Gulielmus potum coxit.

GULIELMUS potum coxit,
  Robert' ergo et Allani :
Noctu tres hilariores,
  Fuerunt non in Christandie.
    Non inebriamur nos,
      Scintilla tantum oculo :
    Canat gallus—luceat :
      Lætabimur in poculo.

Joviales tres sedemus
  Tres sedemus ebrii,
Beatas noctes vidimus,
  Speramus pluribus frui.
    Nos inebriamur, etc.

Ecce cornua lunellæ,
  Nitentis illuc quantulum !
Tentat trahere ad domum,
  Pol ! restabit tantulum.
    Nos inebriamur, etc.

51

Wha first shall rise to gang awa',
A cuckold coward loon is he!
Wha last beside his chair shall fa',
He is the king amang us three!
We are na fou, etc.

Ille primus qui exsurget,
  Cuccurra timidissime !
Qui sub sella primus cadet,
  Trium nostrum rex ille.
    Nos inebriamur, etc.

Somebody.

MY heart is sair—I dare na tell,—
    My heart is sair for somebody;
I could wake a winter night
    For the sake o' somebody.
        Oh-hon! for somebody!
        Oh-hey! for somebody!
    I could range the world around,
        For the sake o' somebody!

Ye powers that smile on virtuous love,
    O, sweetly smile on somebody!
Frae ilka danger keep him free,
    And send me safe my somebody.
        Oh-hon! for somebody!
        Oh-hey! for somebody!
    I wad do—what wad I not?
        For the sake of somebody!

Ægrotus sum—non indicem.

ÆGROTUS sum—non indicem—
   Agrotus sum ob quempiam ;
Totam noctem vigilem
   Causam ob cujuspiam.
      Oh! pro unoquopiam,
      Oh! pro unoquopiam,
Orbem circumcurrerem,
Causam ob cujuspiam.

Qui amorem honoratis
   Arrideatis cuipiam,
Molestiam illi vos dematis
   Et date salvum quempiam.
      Oh! pro unoquopiam,
      Oh! pro unoquopiam,
Agerem! quid non agam ?
Causam ob cujuspiam.

This is no my ain Lassie.

THIS is no my ain lassie,
 Fair tho' the lassie be ;
O weel ken I my ain lassie,
 Kind love is in her e'e.

I see a form, I see a face,
Ye weel may wi' the fairest place :
It wants, to me, the witching grace,
 The kind love that's in her e'e.
  O this is, etc.

She's bonnie, blooming, straight, and tall,
And lang has had my heart in thrall ;
And aye it charms my very saul,
 The kind love that's in her e'e.
  O this is, etc.

A thief sae pawkie is my Jean,
To steal a blink, by a' unseen ;
But gleg as light are lovers' een,
 When kind love is in the e'e.
  O this is, etc.

O hæc non mi puellula.

HÆC non mi puellula,
   Pulchra quamvis sit illa,
Nosco mi puellulam,
   Amor est in oculo.

Formam faciem video,
Dignam loco principe,
Eget dulci decore,
   Amore ejus oculo.
     O hæc non, etc.

Pulchra, recta, florida,
Me tenuit mancipio,
Delectat semper animum,
   Amor ejus oculo.
     O hæc non, etc.

Furuncula versuta est
Furari visum secretò,
Sed agiles rivales hi
   Quum amor sit in oculo.
     O hæc non, etc.

It may escape the courtly sparks,
It may escape the learned clerks ;
But weel the watching lover marks
The kind love that's in her e'e.
      O this is, etc.

Evadat bene aulicis,
Evadat atque clerico,
Sed notat alter vigilans
  Amorem qui in oculo.
    O hæc non, etc.

Last May a braw Wooer.

LAST May a braw wooer cam' down the lang glen,
  And sair wi' his love he did deave me ;
I said there was naething I hated like men,
  The deuce gae wi'm, to believe me, believe me,
  The deuce gae w'im, to believe me !

He spak' o' the darts in my bonnie black een,
  And vow'd for my love he was dying ;
I said he might die when he liked, for Jean,
  The Lord forgi'e me for lying, for lying,
  The Lord forgi'e me for lying.

A weel-stocked mailen,—himsel' for the laird,—
  And marriage aff-hand, were his proffers :
I never loot on that I kenn'd it, or car'd,
  But thought I might ha'e waur offers, waur offers,
  But thought I might ha'e waur offers.

But what wad ye think ? in a fortnight or less,—
  The deil tak' his taste to gae near her !
He up the lang loan to my black cousin Bess,
  Guess ye how, the jad ! I could bear her, could bear her,
  Guess ye how, the jad ! I could bear her.

𝔐𝔞𝔦𝔬, 𝔞𝔪𝔞𝔱𝔬𝔯 𝔟𝔢𝔫𝔦𝔱 𝔭𝔢𝔯 𝔟𝔞𝔩𝔩𝔢𝔪.

——

MAIO, amator venit per vallem,
  Et amore me multo pertusit,
Hominibus, dixi, odisse nil pejus !
    Sed malum ! ut ille mi crederet crederet
    Sed malum ! ut ille mi crederet.

De telis, et dixit, oculorum meorum
  Et amore se tunc moriturum.
Moreretur, respondi, si placet pro me,
    Absolvite, dii ! mendacem mendacem
    Absolvite, dii ! mendacem.

Prædium instructum, ipse dominus,
  Et nuptiæ conditiones !
Non ei impertivi ut curaverim,
    Sed censui essent pejores pejores
    Sed censui essent pejores.

Quid sentias nunc ? ille paulo post hæc,
  Sensum mal' ! ut appropinquareret,
Inconstans ad Betham direct' abiit,
    Conjice ! quàm illam paterer paterer
    Conjice ! quàm illam paterer.

61

But a' the niest week as I fretted wi' care,
  I gaed to the tryste o' Dalgarnock,
And wha but my fine fickle lover was there!
  I glowr'd as I'd seen a warlock, a warlock,
  I glowr'd as I'd seen a warlock.

But owre my left shouther I ga'e him a blink,
  Lest neebors might say I was saucy;
My wooer he caper'd as he'd been in drink,
  And vow'd I was his dear lassie, dear lassie,
  And vow'd I was his dear lassie.

I spier'd for my cousin fu' couthy and sweet,
  Gin she had recover'd her hearin',
And how her new shoon fit her auld shach'lt feet,
  But, heavens! how he fell a swearin', a swearin',
  But, heavens! how he fell a swearin'.

He begged, for gudesake! I wad be his wife,
  Or else I wad kill him wi' sorrow:
So e'en to preserve the poor body in life,
  I think I maun wed him to-morrow, to-morrow,
  I think I maun wed him to-morrow.

Hebdomada, anxi me ex animo,
  Trinundini ludos adibam ;
Et quis ni amator obstaret mihi ?
  Vidit ! ac si viderit magiam magiam
  Vidit ! ac si viderit magiam.

Sed lente recedens connixi illi,
  Ne quis me putaret protervam :
Exsultat amator, ac si ebrius,
  Et vovit me suam puellam puellam
  Et vovit me suam puellam.

De Betha rogavi adeo suaviter,
  Si auditus recuperaretur,
Quam aptarint me' soleæ loripedi.
  Dii ! quàm ille imprecaretur-caretur
  Dii ! quàm ille imprecaretur.

Oravit, per Deum, ut essem uxor
  Enecarem vel cum dolore ;
Et tantum tenere in illo vitam
  Mane proximo nubi me volo me volo
  Mane proximo nubi me volo.

Maggie Lauder.

WHA wadna be in love,
   Wi' bonnie Maggie Lauder?
A piper met her gaun to Fife,
   And speir'd what was't they ca'd her;—
Right scornfully she answered him,
   Begone, you hallanshaker!
Jog on your gate, you bladderskate,
   My name is Maggie Lauder.

Maggie, quo he, and by my bags,
   I'm fidgin fain to see thee;
Sit down by me, my bonnie bird,
   In troth I winnie steer thee:
For I'm a piper to my trade,
   My name is Rob the Ranter;
The lassies loup as they were daft
   When I blaw up my chanter.

Piper, quo Meg, ha'e ye your bags?
   Or is your drone in order?
If ye be Rob, I've heard of you,
   Live you upo' the border.

Quis bir non affectus sit?

QUIS vir non affectus sit
  Ab Maggea Lauder?
Roganti quæ tibicini
  Qui appellaretur.
Respondit ei ironicè :
  "Discede hallinshaker ;
Abscede heus ! tu bletherscate :
  Sum Maggea Lauder."

Tunc ille : "per utriculum !
  Dispereo te videre;
Adside me, carissima !
  Vim nolo adhibere ;
Tibicen, mea arte, sum,
  Robertus Gloriosus ;
Puellæ saltant leviter
  Cum ego sum ventosus."

Maggea tunc : "Tibicen
  An tibi sunt utriculi,
Robertus si, de te novi ;
  Vivisne super termino ?

The lasses a', baith far and near,
    Have heard o' Rob the Ranter;
I'll shake my foot wi' right gude will,
    Gif you'll blaw up your chanter.

Then to his bags he flew wi' speed,
    About the drone he twisted;
Meg up and wallop'd o'er the green,
    For brawly could she frisk it.
Weel done! quo' he—Play up! quo' she;
    Weel bobb'd! quo' Rob the Ranter;
'Tis worth my while to play indeed,
    When I ha'e sic a dancer.

Weel ha'e ye play'd your part, quo' Meg,
    Your cheeks are like the crimson;
There's nane in Scotland plays sae weel,
    Since we lost Habbie Simpson.
I've liv'd in Fife, baith maid and wife,
    These ten years and a quarter;
Gin ye should come to Anster fair,
    Speir ye for Maggie Lauder.

Terrarum orbis puellis
 Robertulus est notus:
Saltabo libentissimè
 Sufflas si gloriosus."

Utriculos nunc adripit,
 Et circiter contorsit,
Saltavit illa gramine,
 Nam pertripudiaret.
" Euge !" ille "suffla !" illa
 Tunc ille Gloriosus :
" Est flaro pretium operæ
 Tal' ergo saltatoris."

" Cecinisti ben'," illa
 " Similes cocco genæ :
Nullus Scotus ludat sic
 A tempore Simpsoni.
Fifensis virg' et uxor sum
 Decennium cum quarto ;
Si venis apud Ansterum,
 Roga de Magge' Lauder."

How long and dreary is the Night.

———

NOW long and dreary is the night,
　　When I am frae my dearie?
I restless lie frae e'en to morn,
　　Tho' I were ne'er sae weary.
　　　　For oh, her lanely nights are lang;
　　　　　And oh, her dreams are eerie;
　　　　　And oh, her widow'd heart is sair,
　　　　　That's absent frae her dearie.

When I think on the lightsome days
　　I spent wi' thee, my dearie;
And now what seas between us roar,—
　　How can I be but eerie?

How slow ye move, ye heavy hours;
　　The joyless day how dreary!
It was na sae ye glinted by,
　　When I was wi' my dearie.
　　　　For oh, her lanely nights are lang;
　　　　　And oh, her dreams are eerie;
　　　　　And oh, her widow'd heart is sair,
　　　　　That's absent frae her dearie.

68

Quam longa nox et lugubris!

QUAM longa nox et lugubris!
　　Absente meo caro,
Insomnis sæpe jaceo
　　Utcunque fatigata.
　　　Oh! ejus noctes longæ sunt,
　　　Et ejus somnia atra,
　　　Et ejus cor conterritum,
　　　　Absente ejus caro.

Revolvens dies hilares
　　Perductos cum me' caro,
Et mare fremens inter nos
　　Qui possim non mærere.
　　　Oh! ejus noctes, etc.

Quam horae hae tardipedes!
　　Quam luctuosæ horæ!
Heu aliter alipedes
　　Adstante meo caro!
　　　Oh! ejus noctes longæ sunt,
　　　Et ejus somnia atra,
　　　Et ejus cor conterritum
　　　　Absente ejus caro.

My Spouse, Nancy.

USBAND, husband, cease your strife,
 No longer idly rave, sir ;
Tho' I am your wedded wife,
 Yet I am not your slave, sir.

HE.

" One of two must still obey,
 Nancy, Nancy ;
Is it man, or woman, say ;
 My spouse, Nancy ?"

SHE.

If 'tis still the lordly word,
 Service and obedience ;
I'll desert my sov'reign lord,
 And so, good b'ye, allegiance.

HE.

" Sad will I be, so bereft,
 Nancy, Nancy,
Yet I'll try to make a shift,
 My spouse, Nancy."

Marite rixas desine.

ARITE rixas desine,
  Nec ineptè desipe :
Licet tua uxor
  Non sum tua servula.

ILLE.

Oportet unum obedire
  Uxor muliercula !
Sive vir aut mulier
  Sponsa mea Nancia !

ILLA.

Si sit verbum arrogans
  Servitium ! servitium.!
Magistrum ego deseram,
  Val' obedientia.

ILLE.

Dolebo sic relictus,
  Uxor muliercula !
Ægre ut perficiam,
  Sponsa mea Nancia.

71

SHE.

My poor heart then break it must,
    My last hour I'm near it :
When you lay me in the dust,
    Think, think, how you will bear it.

HE.

" I will hope and trust in heaven,
    Nancy, Nancy ;
Strength to bear it will be given,
    My spouse, Nancy."

SHE.

Well, sir, from the silent dead,
    Still I'll try to daunt you ;
Ever round your midnight bed
    Horrid sprites shall haunt you.

HE.

" I'll wed another, like my dear
    Nancy, Nancy ;
Then all hell will fly for fear,
    My spouse, Nancy."

ILLÀ.

Meum cor nunc fractum est
  Prope horam ultimam :
Ah ! cogita quam feras
  Quum pones me in terram?

ILLE.

Fidem pono in cœlo
  Uxor muliercula !
Acquiram robur ex eo
  Sponsa mea Nancia.

ILLA.

Bene ! sed ex mortuis
  Conarer te terrere,
Infestabit spiritus
  Nocte circum torum.

ILLE.

Nubam alteri simili
  Uxor muliercula !
Tunc fugient diaboli
  Sponsa mea Nancia.

Fair Jenny.

WHERE are the joys I have met in the morning,
    That danc'd to the lark's early song?
Where is the peace that awaited my wand'ring,
    At evening the wild woods among?

No more a-winding the course of yon river,
    And marking sweet flowerets so fair:
No more I trace the light footsteps of pleasure,
    But sorrow and sad sighing care.

Is it that summer's forsaken our valleys,
    And grim surly winter is near?
No, no! the bees, humming around the gay roses,
    Proclaim it the pride of the year.

Fain would I hide what I fear to discover,
    Yet long, long too well have I known,
All that has caused this wreck in my bosom,
    Is Jenny, fair Jenny alone.

74

Hacc ubi gaudia fulgentis Aurorae.

———

ÆC ubi gaudia fulgentis Auroræ
    Saltantia alaudæ carmini ?
Ubi pax illa me comitans pervagum
    Sylvarum sub umbra vespere ?

Sequar non amplius rivuli flexus
    Et flosculum perclarum notans,
Nil amplius consequar vestigiis amorum :
    Nunc dolor et cura spirans.

Estne ut æstas abdicarit convalles ?
    Et hyems persæva propè ?
Parum ! nam apis susurrus per rosas
    Primulam proclamat anni.

Velim velare quod retegere nolim
    Hoc optime autem novi,
Ut omne quod corde pacem expellat
    Est ILLA et illa sola.

75

Time cannot aid me, my griefs are immortal,
Nor hope dare a comfort bestow :
Come then, enamour'd and fond of my anguish,
Enjoyment I'll seek in my wo.

Non adjuvet tempus ; eternæ me' curæ,
  Nec præbet spes solatium ;
Adesto ! angoris me' inamoratus
  In luctibus me' gaudia quæram.

See the Smoking Bowl.

SEE the smoking bowl before us,
　　Mark our jovial ragged ring;
Round and round take up the chorus,
　　And in raptures let us sing:
　　　　A fig for those by law protected!
　　　　Liberty's a glorious feast!
　　　　Courts for cowards were erected,
　　　　　　Churches built to please the priest.

What is title? what is treasure?
　　What is reputation's care?
If we lead a life of pleasure,
　　'Tis no matter how or where!
　　　　A fig, etc.

With the ready trick and fable,
　　Round we wander all the day;
And at night, in barn or stable,
　　Hug our doxies on the hay.
　　　　A fig, etc.

Ecce scyphus coram nobis!

ECCE scyphus coram nobis!
　　Potatorum gaudium,
Et per omnes eat chorus
　　Nos canamus canticum.
　　　Habeo nihili legales
　　　　Gloriosa libertas!
　　　Sunt curiæ pro timidis
　　　　Ecclesiæ et clericis.

Quid titulus? divitiæ?
　　Fama quid? aut gloria?
Si agemus vitam dulcem
　　Quid descrimen qui aut qua?
　　　Habeo, etc.

Dolo et cum fabula
　　Vagamur nos quotidie,
Horreo aut stabulo
　　Concubimus in stramine.
　　　Habeo, etc.

79

Does the train-attended carriage
    Thro' the country lighter rove?
Does the sober bed of marriage
    Witness brighter scenes of love?
        A fig, etc.

Life is all a variorum,
    We regard not how it goes;
Let them cant about decorum
    Who have characters to lose.
        A fig, etc.

Here's to budgets, bags, and wallets!
    Here's to all the wandering train!
Here's our ragged brats and callets!
    One and all cry out, Amen!
        A fig, etc.

Dic mi et num currus grandis
  Via vadat levior?
Dic mi num in sancto toro
  Amor sit lucidior?
    Habeo, etc.

Vita tantum variorum :
  Non curamus vadat qua;
Cantanto morem perdecorum
  Quibus cara est fama.
    Habeo, etc.

Salutem peris tunc potemus
  Gregi vago salutem :
Infantulis et scortulis
  Clamatote vos Amen !
    Habeo, etc.

I hae a wife o' my ain.

I HAE a wife o' my ain—
  I'll partake wi' nae-body;
I'll tak' cuckold frae nane,
  I'll gi'e cuckold to nae-body.

I ha'e a penny to spend,
  There—thanks to naebody;
I ha'e naething to lend,
  I'll borrow frae nae-body.

I am nae-body's lord—
  I'll be a slave to nae-body;
I hae a guid braid sword,
  I'll tak' dunts frae nae-body.

I'll be merry and free,
  I'll be sad for nae-body;
If nae-body care for me,
  I'll care for naebody.

Est mulier unico mi.

ST mulier unico mi,
 Participo cum nemine,
Currucam nemini sumam,
 Dabo currucam nemini.

Mihi denarius est;
 Ecce! gratias nemini;
Ad fœnus habeo nil,
 Sumam nihilum alicui.

Dominus neminis sum,
 Servus ero nemini,
Gladius longus mi,
 Patiar plagas neminis.

Liber et ero hilăris,
 Tristis propter neminem,
Si nemo curet me,
 Ego curabo neminem.

O whistle, and I'll come to you, my Lad.

WHISTLE, and I'll come to you, my lad,
   O whistle, and I'll come to you, my lad;
   Tho' father and mither and a' should gae mad,
   O whistle, and I'll come to you, my lad.

But warily tent, when you come to court me,
And come nae unless the back-yett be a-jee;
Syne up the back-stile and let naebody see,
And come as ye were na comin' to me.
       O whistle, etc.

At kirk, or at market, whene'er ye meet me,
Gang by me as though ye car'd na a flie;
But steal me a blink o' your bonnie black e'e,
Yet look as ye were na lookin' at me.
       O whistle, etc.

Aye vow and protest that ye care na for me,
And whyles ye may lightly my beauty a wee;
But court na anither, though jokin' ye be,
For fear that she wyle your fancy frae me.
       O whistle, etc.

Fistula! adsum, jubenis me.

FISTÚLA! adsum, juvenis mi,
Fistula! adsum, juvenis mi,
Delirent parentes et alii,
Fistula! adsum, juvenis mi.

Sed cave si ambiens viseris me,
Non nisi sit janua de obice,
Posticam per portam furlivè repe
Cum nullus vicinus videat te.
    Fistula! etc.

Quand' apud nundinas sim visa tibi,
Me prætori ac si essem nihili;
Tautum emicet jactus tuæ acici,
Sed adspice ac si non adspicis me.
    Fistula, etc.

Tunc vove te non curare pro me,
Et faciem meam habere flocci;
Sed jocosè non ambito alteram—ne
Tuum amorem auferat mi.
    Fistula! etc.

Bruce's Address to his Army.

SCOTS, wha ha'e wi' Wallace bled;
Scots, wham Bruce has aften led;
Welcome to your gory bed,
    Or to glorious victorie !

Now's the day, and now's the hour ;—
See the front o' battle lower ;
See approach proud Edward's power—
    Edward ! chains and slaverie !

Wha will be a traitor knave ?
Wha can fill a coward's grave ?
Wha sae base as be a slave ?
    Traitor ! coward ! turn and flee !

Wha for Scotland's king and law
Freedom's sword will strongly draw,
Freeman stand or freeman fa',
    Sodger ! hero ! on wi' me !

Commilites Wallacio.

———

COMMILITES Wallacio;
Scoti ducti Brucio;
Cruento grati lectulo!
  Mors aut victoria!

Nunc hora est nunc dies,
En! prima prœlii acies!
Nunc accedunt Saxones
  Edwardus, vincula!

Quisne erit perfidus?
Quis morietur pavidus?
Servus quis ignobilis?
  Ignave! fugito!.

Legem et qui regem amat,
Et pro iis ensem trahat
Liber vivat, liber cadat:
  Instetis vos cum me.

By oppression's woes and pains !
By your sons in servile chains,
We will drain our dearest veins,
    But they shall be—shall be free !

Lay the proud usurpers low !
Tyrants fall in every foe !
Liberty's in every blow!
    Forward ! let us do, or die !

Pœnas per tyrannidis,
Per filios in vinculis,
Expertes simus sanguinis,
　Erĭmus liberi !

Sternite tyrannos hos
Pernumeratos ictibus ;
In omni plaga libertas !
　Est Scotis vincere !

Up in the morning's no for me.

U P in the morning's no for me,
  Up in the morning early :
When a' the hills are covered wi' snaw,
  I'm sure it's winter fairly.

Cauld blaws the wind frae east to west,
  The drift is driving sairly ;
Sae loud and shrill I hear the blast,
  I'm sure it's winter fairly.
      Up in the morning, etc.

The birds sit chittering in the thorn,
  A' day they fare but sparely ;
And lang's the night frae e'en to morn,—
  I'm sure it's winter fairly.
      Up in the morning, etc.

Surgere mane mordet me.

———

SURGERE manè mordet me,
Surgere lectulo manè,
Omnes colles teguntur nive ;
Ecce! hiemat planè.

Subsolanus frigidè flat
Et nivium vis immanè,
Canorus ventus ejulat;
Ecce! hiemat planè.
    Surgere, etc.

Aviculis tremulis in spinis,
Sunt paucissima grana,
Atra nox perlonga est;
Ecce! hiemat planè.
    Surgere, etc.

Here awa, there awa, wandering Willie.

—

HERE awa, there awa, wandering Willie,
   Now tired with wandering, haud awa hame !
Come to my bosom, my ae only dearie,
   And tell me thou bring'st me my Willie the same.

Loud blew the cauld winter winds at our parting;
   It was na the blast brought the tear in my e'e :
Now welcome the simmer, and welcome my Willie,
   The simmer to nature, my Willie to me.

Ye hurricanes, rest in the cave o' your slumbers !
   O how your wild horrors a lover alarms !
Awaken ye breezes, row gently ye billows,
   And waft my dear laddie ance mair to my arms.

But if he's forgotten his faithfullest Nannie,
   O still flow between us, thou wide roaring main ;
May I never see it, may I never trow it,
   But, dying, believe that my Willie's my ain!

Adiens, abiens, vagule Guille!

—

ADIENS, abiens, vagule Guille!
  Adiens, abiens domum veni ;
Adés mo' pectori caro mo' Guille ;
  Dic te redire eundem ad me.

Flant hiemis venti, dum nos separamur,
  Me lacrymante pertimidè ;
Adsit nunc æstas! adsit nunc Guille!
  Æstas naturæ, sed Guillus mihi.

Quiescite venti in Æoli antris,
  Quam ululatus perterrent me !
Flate vos auræ! advolvite undulæ!
  Reddite carum mo' Guillum ad me.

Sed oh si inconstans aut mo' obliviscens,
  Volvas in medio tu fremens mare !
Videam nunquam, nec audiam unquam,
  Sed moriens credam fidelem mihi.

93

Macpherson's Farewell.

FAREWELL, ye dungeons dark and strong,
  The wretch's destinie !
Macpherson's time will not be long,
  On yonder gallows-tree.
    Sae rantingly, sae wantonly,
      Sae dauntingly gaed he ;
    He play'd a spring, and danc'd it round,
      Below the gallows-tree.

O what is death but parting breath ?—
  On mony a bloody plain
I've dar'd his face, and in this place
  I scorn him yet again !
    Sae rantingly, etc.

Untie these bands from off my hands,
  And bring to me my sword ;
And there's no a man in all Scotland,
  But I'll brave him at a word.
    Sae rantingly, etc.

Valete atri carceres!

ALETE atri carceres !
    Fatum miserrimo !
Huic breve tempus qui adstat
    Subter patibulo.
        En ! leviter ! alacriter !
        Perfortiter ille
        Et cantat et saltat
        Subter patibulo.

Mors ! modo aura exspirans
    In prœlii campo !
Adspexi ejus faciem,
    Et iterum audeo.
        En ! leviter ! etc.

Solvite manus ipsas mi,
    Da mihi gladium ;
Et vir nullus in Scotia
    Quin verbo obstringam.
        En ! leviter ! etc.

I've liv'd a life of sturt and strife ;
I die by treacherie :
It burns my heart, I must depart
And not avenged be !
Sae rantingly, etc.

Now farewell, light,—thou sunshine bright,
And all beneath the sky !
May coward shame distain his name,
The wretch that dares not die !
Sae rantingly, etc.

Vitam rixosam duxi ;
Morior perfidia ;
Et ferox nunc exuror,
Ut non vindicem me.
En ! leviter ! etc.

Nunc vale lux et clare sol
Omnes adstatis qui !
Sed illi ignominia
Qui metuit mori.
En ! leviter ! etc.

O Lassie, art thou sleeping yet.

O LASSIE, art thou sleeping yet,
Or art thou wakin', I would wit?
For love has bound me hand and foot,
   And I would fain be in, jo.
      O let me in this ae night,
         This ae, ae, ae night;
      For pity's sake this ae night,
         O rise and let me in, jo!

Thou hear'st the winter wind and weet,
Nae star blinks through the driving sleet;
Tak' pity on my weary feet,
   And shield me frae the rain, jo.
      O let, etc.

The bitter blast that round me blaws
Unheeded howls, unheeded fa's;
The cauldness o' thy heart's the cause
   Of a' my grief and pain, jo.
      O let, etc.

An dormis tu birguncula?

ILLE.

N dormis tu virguncula?
Aut vigilas? nam vincula
Amoris circumretiunt me,
Et velim introire—jo.
  Oh! liceat mi hac nocte
  Hac una nocte unicè,
  Causa misericordiæ,
    Oh! liceat mi intrare—jo.

Insanit ventus horridus,
  Stellæque sunt ubivagæ,
Oh! lassi miserere me',
  Sub tectis me defende—jo.
  Oh! liceat, etc.

Heu! mordax ventus qui afflat
  Inscitus cadit, ejulat,
Nam cordis frigus causa est
  Angoris mei omnis—jo.
  Oh! liceat, etc.

HER ANSWER.

O tell na me o' wind and rain,
Upbraid na me wi' cauld disdain !
Gae back the gait ye cam' again,
    I winna let you in, jo.
        I tell you now this ae night,
        This ae, ae, ae night,
        And ance for a' this ae night,
        I winna let you in, jo.

The snellest blast, at mirkest hours,
That round the pathless wand'rer pours,
Is nocht to what poor she endures,
    That's trusted faithless man, jo.
        I tell, etc.

The sweetest flower that deck'd the mead,
Now trodden like the vilest weed ;
Let simple maid the lesson read,
    The weird may be her ain, jo.
        I tell, etc.

The bird that charm'd his summer-day,
Is now the cruel fowler's prey ;
Let witless, trusting, woman say
    How aft her fate's the same, jo.
        I tell, etc.

ILLA.

Dic ne ventos horridos,
  Dicasne supercilia
Et pedes refero tuos
  Non licet introire—jo.
    Dico nam hac nocte,
      Hac una nocte unicè,
      Semel hac in nocte
    Non licet introire—jo.

Nam ventus quem nox induit
  Et viatorem ingruit,
Est nil præ eo quod luit
  Quæ viro semper credit—jo.
    Dico nam, etc.

Flos suavis inter pratula
  Calcatus est ac herbula :
Heu! simplex virgo! legito,
  Fortuna fiat sua—jo.
    Dico nam, etc.

Avicula quæ cantillans,
  Heu! nunc in plicis laquei :
Insipienti virgini,
  Est illi lectioni—jo.
    Dico nam, etc.

A Man's a Man for a' that.

IS there, for honest poverty,
  That hangs his head, and a' that ;
The coward-slave, we pass him by,
  We dare be poor for a' that!
For a' that, and a' that,
  Our toils obscure, and a' that,
The rank is but the guinea's stamp,
  The man's the gowd for a' that.

What tho' on hamely fare we dine,
  Wear hoddin grey, and a' that ;
Gi'e fools their silks, and knaves their wine,
  A man's a man for a' that!
For a' that, and a' that,
  Their tinsel show, and a' that ;
The honest man, though e'er sae poor,
  Is king o' men for a' that!

Ye see yon birkie, ca'd a lord,
  Wha struts, and stares, and a' that ;
Though hundreds worship at his word,
  He's but a coof for a' that :

Estne pro pauperiem.

ESTNE pro pauperiem
 Qui langueat—et omne quid!
To timido! dimittimus
 Egeni nos—et omne quid.
Nihilominus, nihilominus,
 Angustiæ—et omne quid.
Notatum aurum Ordo est,
 Aurum vir—per omne quid.

Licet nobis olera,
 Pannique, aqua—omne quid ;
Da stultis vinum, sericas,
 Vir est vir—per omne quid.
Nihilominus, nihilominus,
 Pompæ, nugæ—omne quid ;
Honestus licet pauper vir
 Rex hominum—per omne quid

Homuncio ecce dominus!
 Qui turgeat—et omne quid ;
Adorent licet sexcenti
 Stultus est—per omne quid.

For a' that, and a' that,
   His riband, star, and a' that,
The man of independent mind,
   He looks and laughs at a' that !

A king can mak' a belted knight,
   A marquis, duke, and a' that ;
But an honest man's aboon his might,
   Guid faith he maunna fa' that !
For a' that, and a' that,
   Their dignities, and a' that,
The pith o' sense, and pride o' worth,
   Are higher ranks than a' that.

Then let us pray that come it may—
   As come it will for a' that—
That sense and worth, o'er a' the earth,
   May bear the gree, and a' that !
For a' that, and a' that,
   It's coming yet for a' that,
That man to man, the warld o'er,
   Shall brothers be for a' that !

Nihilominus, nihilominus,
    Stellæ, vittæ—omne quid;
En vir subjectus nemini
    Arridet ille—omne quid.

Rex facere posset equitem,
    Marchionem, ducem—omne quid ;
Sed vir honestus superat :
    Mehercle! non consummet id.
Nihilominus, nihilominus,
    Et Ordines—et omne quid ;
Mens sana recti conscia
    Excelsior est quam omne quid.

Oremus ergo accidat,
    Et accidet per omne quid ;
Ut probitasque bonitas
    Sint principes—per omne quid.
Nihilominus, nihilominus,
    Venturum est—per omne quid ;
Ut homines hominibus
    Fratres sint—per omne quid.

Dainty Davie.

NOW rosy May comes in wi' flowers,
　To deck her gay, green-spreading bowers ;
And now comes in my happy hours,
　To wander wi' my Davie.
　　Meet me on the warlock knowe,
　　Dainty Davie, dainty Davie ;
　　There I'll spend the day wi' you,
　　My ain dear dainty Davie.

The crystal waters round us fa',
The merry birds are lovers a',
The scented breezes round us blaw,
　A wandering wi' my Davie.
　　Meet me, etc.

When purple morning starts the hare,
·　To steal upon her early fare,
Then thro' the dews I will repair,
　To meet my faithfu' Davie.
　　Meet me, etc.

Nunc venit Maia rosea.

NUNC venit Maia rosea,
Adornans hæc umbracula,
Nunc dies quibus lubet mî
Vaganti cum me' Davo.
Adesto colli lamiæ!
Laute Dave! laute Dave!
Diem agam tunc cum te,
Meus care Dave!

Fontanæ aquæ scintillant,
Amores aves cantillant,
Auræ lenissimæ afflant,
Vagante sic cum Davo.
Adesto, etc.

Cum dies citat leporem,
Ad carpendum pascuum,
Roratam transeo viam,
Ut conveniam Davum.
Adesto, etc.

When day expiring in the west,
The curtain draws o' nature's rest,
I flee to his arms I lo'e best,
    And that's my ain dear Davie.
    Meet me, etc.

Cum sol descendit in mare,
Et cœlum velant tenebræ,
Ad te volo carissime!
  Meus laute Dave.
    Adesto, etc.

Whistle owre the lave o't.

LET me ryke up to dight that tear,
  And go wi' me and be my dear,
  And then your every care and fear
    May whistle owre the lave o't.
      I am a fiddler to my trade,
      And a' the tunes that e'er I play'd,
      The sweetest still to wife or maid,
        Was whistle owre the lave o't.

At kirns and weddings we'se be there,
And O ! sea nicely's we will fare ;
We'll bouse about, till Daddie Care
  Sings whistle owre the lave o't.
    I am, etc.

Sae merrily's the banes we'll pyke,
And sun oursells about the dyke,
And at our leisure, when ye like,
  We'll whistle owre the lave o't.
    I am, etc.

But bless me wi' your heav'n o' charms,
And while I kittle hair on thairms,
Hunger, cauld, and a' sic harms,
  May whistle owre the lave o't
    I am, etc.

Hanc lacrymam abstergeamue.

ANC lacrymam abstergeamue,
Et vade mecum cara mi,
Et omnes curæ metusque,
  Fistulent etcetera.
    Tibicen Ego arte me',
    Modorum semper quos lusi
    Suavissimus hic ubique,
      Est fistula etcetera.

Ad nuptialia ibimus,
Et oh! opòpàro bibemus
Curas sonis coagemus,
  Fistulent etcetera.
    Tibicen Ego, etc.

Carnem ex ossibus rodemus
Ut juxta fossulas solemus,
Et ubi placeat ludemus
  " Fistula etcetera."
    Tibicen Ego, etc.

Beato lenociniis me,
Dum cano canticum suave,
Et frigus, fames, apage!
  Fistulent etcetera.
    Tibicen Ego, etc.

By Rev. Geo. C. Lorrimer, D. D,

Should auld acquaintance be forgot
  And never brought to min'?
Should we forget the auld thatched cot
  And days o' lang syne ?
For auld lang syne, my dear,
  For auld lang syne,
We'll tak' a taought o' kindness yet
  For auld lang syne.

We twa hae run about the braes
  And pu't the gowan's fine,
But we've wondered mony weary days
  Sin' auld lang syne.
For auld lang syne, my dear,
  For auld lang syne.
We'll tak' a thought o' kindness yet
  For auld lang syne.

We twa hae pa'dl't i' the the brook
  Frae mornin' sun till dine,
And play'd aroun' the ingle nook,
  In auld lang syne.
For auld lang syne, my dear,
  For auld lang syne,
We'll tak' a thought o' kindness yet
  For auld lang syne.

Still daises fair and heather bell
  Deck banks a' sweet wi' thyme,
But cauld the heart we lo'ed sa well,
  In auld lang syne.
For auld lang syne, my dear,
  For auld lang syne,
We'll tak' a thought o' kindness yet
  For auld lang syne.

Let present years be bright and gay,
  And flowers our brow entwine,
That ne'er can bring a sunnier day
  Than auld lang syne.
For auld lang syne, my dear,
  For auld lang syne,
We'll tak' a thought o' kindness yet
  For auld lang syne.

We need na' surely a pint stoup
  To cheer your heart and mine,
Nor sparkling wine on which to look
  For auld lang syne.
For auld lang syne, my dear,
  For auld lang syne,
We'll tak' a though o' kindness yet
  For auld lang syne.

And here's a hand my trustie friend,
  And gie's a hand o' thine,
And let our hearts in friendship blend,
  For auld lang syne.
For auld lang syne, my dear,
  For auld lang syne,
We'll tak' a thought o' kindness yet
  For auld lang syne.
                    --The Watchman.

THE

COTTAGE YOUTH;

OR,

WILLIAM BALL.

LONDON:
THE RELIGIOUS TRACT SOCIETY;
56, PATERNOSTER ROW; 65, ST. PAUL'S CHURCHYARD;
AND 164, PICCADILLY:
AND SOLD BY THE BOOKSELLERS.

No. 1615.

COTTAGE YOUTH.

THE sun has seldom turn'd his face
To smile upon a lovelier place
Than Dunlop hill; fresh, fair, and dry,
It fronts the south and western sky;
The trees in wild luxuriance grow,
And pure the evening breezes blow.

The landscape round is fair to see,
The parsonage, and chestnut-tree,
The blacksmith's shop, the parish
    pound,
The windmill, whirling round and
    round,
The flowing brook, the trickling rills,
The cottages, and towering hills
That many a ridge and peak display,
And in the distance die away.
Sure never yet did jackdaw perch
Upon a prettier parish church
Than that whose glittering spire is
    seen
Right opposite the village green;
Nor twittering swallows skim around
A neater cot and garden ground
Than, take the place for all in all,
The happy home of William Ball.

But let us now go back to shew
What happened forty years ago;
To tell, in words of sober truth,
The narrative of William's youth;
His birth, his parentage, and all
That did in years gone by befall.

Old Roger, William's father, still
Lives at the cot beyond the mill,
Where the big oak-tree throws abroad
Its spreading branches o'er the road.
His father's father, blithe and free,
Has gathered acorns from the tree;
And sometimes Roger boasts, e'en
    now,
That he has climbed up every bough.
Now Roger Ball and his good dame,
Though poor, possess'd an honest
    fame;

For all the neighbours round could
    raise
Their voices loud in Phœbe's praise;
And oft the rustic phrase would fall,
"As honest, ay, as Roger Ball!"

Three children had they in their day,
But two of them were called away;
Their dust was laid where all must go,
The rich and poor, the high and low.
The weeping parents in their grief,
Resigned, look'd upward for relief:
They saw and felt what death had
    done,
And yearned towards their only son.
That son was William; taught with
    care
To bend his knees in praise and
    prayer,
To trust in God in joy and smart,
And love the Lord with all his heart,
He grew in years and graces, still
Obey'd with joy his parents' will,
And gladly did his best to prove
His filial duty and his love.

With many a wise and thoughtful
    rule
They sent him to the Sunday school,
That he might prosper on his way
In grace and knowledge day by day;
And go where plainly might be heard
The truths of God's most holy word;
Truths that, once learn'd, will ne'er
    depart,
But dwell for ever in the heart.
The lessons William learn'd were
    blest,
And deeply sank within his breast,
And fill'd his soul with godly fear,
And dried up many a falling tear.
How many a man, who, once a wild,
Unlovely, disobedient child,
Refused his parents to obey
Till wise instruction smooth'd the
    way,

Repress'd his passions, clipp'd his
    wings,
And led him on to heavenly things,—
Now owns, while humbler paths are
    trod,
That sabbath schools are gifts from
    God.

Oh best asylums! thoughtless youth
Imbibe in them the words of truth ;
And learn to love the Lord and pray,
And look on Jesus as the way,
The only way that God has given
Whereby a sinner enters heaven.

Though kind affections seem'd to
    reign
In William's bosom, it was plain
A hasty temper dwelt within,
And this was his besetting sin ;
A sin that cost him many a tear,
And call'd for many an earnest prayer.

Roger, before the rising sun
His race of glory had begun,
Before the lark was in the sky,
Whate'er the weather, wet or dry,
With William rose : they left their bed
To gain by toil their daily bread.
'Twas Roger's task the plough to
    guide,
While William whistled at his side.

Thus things went on without a
    change ;
And still they worked at Lifford
    Grange ;
But in the lives that seemed to pass
Unruffled, and as smooth as glass,
Unlook'd-for things at times befall.
It happen'd that at Broughton Hall
They wanted all at once to find
A youngster of a willing mind ;
A handy lad to fetch the news,
To clean the knives, to brush the shoes,
To weed the walks, well roil'd and
    wide,
And do a hundred jobs beside.
The servant-man call'd in to say
That Jenkins had been turned away ;
Sent off in haste in sad disgrace,
And William Ball might have the
    place.

When Roger heard the news, he
    stood
Awhile, then spoke in hopeful mood :
" Bill, you shall go : such places, lad,
" May not be always to be had.
" Keep up your heart, for who can tell
" What may betide if things go well ?
" We purblind mortals little know
" What God in mercy can bestow :
" This offer'd place at Broughton Hall
" May prove a blessing to us all.
" Right little good is got, I fear,
" By changing places hereand there,
" And I should think that one in ten
" Would hardly suit the Squire ; but
    then,
" In things most difficult, they say,
" The Will will always find a way
" A ready hand and good intent
" In service are most excellent.
" Be honest still, though you are poor,
" And hark ye ! when you go, be sure
" You do your best, and never shun
" What duty tells you should be done.
" Let neither worldly joys nor cares
" Tempt you with all their various
    snares,
" To break the sabbath. Look above,
" In trouble, to a God of love,
" And seek his grace in prayer and
    praise,
" That he may guide you all your
    days.
" Your temper's rather hot and strong,
" So keep a bridle on your tongue :
" Use no bad words, call no hard
    names ;
" A spark may set a house in flames.
" And let your fellow-servants find
" That you can do with ready mind
" Whate'er your master may require ;
" Squire Wright is a right worthy
    squire."
Here Roger left, and William stood
Awhile in melancholy mood,
Reflecting on his future place ;
And when with careful, anxious face,
His mother ask'd him why he sigh'd
And look'd so sad ? he thus replied—
" To speak the truth, I'd rather still
" Keep on my frock the ground to till ;
" My father's father held the plough,
" Content my father holds it now ;

" And I, with every rising sun,
" Would spend my days as they have
      done.
" But if it must be so, it must,
" And all will turn out well, I trust.
" At any rate, the Squire shall find
" A ready hand and willing mind :
" With this continual wish possest,
" As father says, to do my best."

That night, when Roger knelt in
      prayer,
With humble heart he spread his care
At once before th' Eternal throne,
And, in the name of Christ alone,
Implored that God would watch their
      ways,
That they might still show forth his
      praise,
And William guide, and keep and bless
In paths of truth and holiness.
In heartfelt prayer the troubled find
A load is taken from the mind :
The crooked is made straight and
      clear,
And the rough places plain appear :
Just so it proved with Roger Ball,
And this will be the case with all.
And William, too, with anxious care,
And burden'd heart, put up a prayer,
And soon, like clouds at break of day,
His fears and troubles pass'd away.

The stars were bright, the moon
      arose,
The tranquil hours of sweet repose
Pass'd smoothly by, and all around
A grateful silence reign'd profound.
The morrow came, and William Ball
Walk'd slowly up to Broughton
      Hall.
Squire Wright was rich in worldly
      store,
And felt content, and that was more.
Frank-hearted, generous, and free,
In word and deed, he loved to see
His servants with a smiling face,
Cheerful and happy in their place ;
But then his worldly course he trod,
A stranger to that peace of God,
Which hope, and joy, and comfort
      brings,
And finds delight in heavenly things.

How rich is he, whose grateful eyes
Can wander o'er the bright blue skies,
O'er heaven's bright arch with plea-
      sure roam,
And say, " It is my Father's home !
Where I shall dwell in peace, and see
His lovely face who died for me !"
While he, alas ! who has no more
Than well-fill'd bags of golden ore,
Prepared alone for this world's need,
With all his wealth is poor indeed.

The boy who does his duty still
With modesty and right good will
Whose hand is ever ready found
To render help to all around,
Is sure a character to raise,
And gain at once respect and praise.
And so it was with William Ball
When errand-lad at Broughton Hall.
The months went round, and day and
      night
His prospects seem'd to get more
      bright,
Till rising in his service higher,
He grew a favourite with the Squire.
No more he went to fetch the news,
Nor clean'd the knives nor brush'd
      the shoes ;
But stood, array'd in livery fair,
To wait behind his master's chair.
It may be thought that such a course,
So fair and smooth, might prove a
      source
Of bitterness, of pain and smart,
By lifting up with pride his heart ;
But changes William meekly bore,
And was as humble as before.
At first he felt a kind of dread
To wear a dress of brown and red ;
It look'd too flaunting, fine and free,
For such a country lad as he ;
But when his fears his father knew,
He thus advised him what to do.
" Ne'er mind it, lad ! a strip of red
" Will neither hurt the heart nor head.
" In what his service may require
" With willing mind obey the Squire.
" It matters not what clothes we wear
" In this vain world of grief and care,
" For all must soon give up their
      breath
" To wear the livery of death.

" Put on the clothes that suit your
place,
" But never stain them with disgrace.
" Your duty do in every part,
" And still preserve an upright heart."

It seemed to brighten up the life
Of Roger Ball and his good wife,
To see their son in such a place,
To mark with joy his prosperous
race;
And, more than all, to know his mind
To vital godliness inclined.

Oh what a soothing, heavenly balm
Has piety the heart to calm!
When once a sense of sin has press'd
Its burden on the sorrowing breast;
And love Divine allay'd the smart,
And fill'd with hope the aching heart;
The grateful spirit upward springs,
With reverence deep for holy things,
And finds, when earthly griefs are
given,
A hope, a joy, a home in heaven.

Time roll'd away, as roll it will,
And all affairs went smoothly still,
For William, on his duty bent,
Still gave his master full content.
But oft when least expected spreads
A threat'ning cloud above our heads;
The angry skies put on a frown,
And suddenly the storm comes down.

When William went to Broughton
Hall,
He promised, let what would befall,
To have his father's words in sight,
To pray to God each morn and night;
The Bible humbly to obey,
And holy keep the sabbath day.
And William held his promise dear:
The time of trial now was near.

It happen'd in the summer time,
When trees and flowers are in their
prime,
Old Ephraim Reed, whose sight was
dim,
Required some help his walks to trim;
The Squire expected friends to call,
And pass some days at Broughton
Hall;

And William had command to stay
And help him all the sabbath day.
Some servants think it a disgrace,
And pertly cry " 'Tis not my place!"
When ask'd to do a trifling thing,
To lift or carry, take or bring,
If such a service should break through
The notions they're accustomed to;
'Tis thus with some, but not with all:
It was not so with William Ball.
He gladly would have trimm'd the
lawn
On Monday at the peep of dawn,
And gone through all the pleasure
ground,
And cleaned and swept the walks
around.
But no; the Squire would have his
way,
And make him work on God's own
day.
In vain he sued and humbly bow'd;
The Squire was positive and proud,
Required at once a Yes or No—
And said that he should work or go.
Thus, at the last, poor William Ball
Was turn'd away from Broughton
Hall.

When this unwelcome news was
known,
A gloom o'er Roger's cot was thrown,
And every heart was fill'd with fears:
That sabbath was a day of tears!
But they were servants of the Lord,
And found him faithful to his word;
Cast down and humbled to the dust,
In God alone they put their trust.
And he in pity sent relief,
And gave them comfort in their
grief.
Said Roger Ball, " Let come what will,
" A throne of grace is left us still;
" A chasten'd child in every case
" Should humbly seek his Father's
face.
" Let us then meekly bear the rod,
" And still adore the Lord our God,
" Who gave his Son, oh wondrous
love,
" To die that we might reign above.
" His matchless mercy none can tell:
" Be patient! All will yet be well."

ONE Harry Strong at Broughton Hall
Fill'd up the place of William Ball;
In changing Ball for Harry Strong,
Squire Wright soon found his judg-
        ment wrong.
No worthless waster might be found
Idling the quiet village round,
No scape-grace near was known to
        dwell,
But thoughtless Harry knew him
        well;
And thus such knaves as cared for
        nought,
In turn to Broughton Hall were
        brought.
By bad example made perverse,
The servants all grew worse and
        worse;
Till e'en the Squire was heard one
        day,
When muttering to himself, to say,—
"A set of idle knaves! Will Ball,
"Say what you may, is worth them all."

Strong went away, and Tomkins came;
The rude disorder was the same.
And after Tomkins, Edward Town,
Put on, in vain, the red and brown;
For every change was bad, alas!
Things came at last to such a pass,
The Squire, though proud, was fain
        to bend,
And Roger was desired to send

His son; so once more William Ball
Took his old place at Broughton
        Hall.
What we for conscience' sake endure
Will turn out well at last, be sure:
The Squire grew kinder than before,
And valued William more and more;
And never after bade him stay
To trim the walks on God's own day.

Time pass'd away, and William grew
In age and reputation too.
Humble and pious and sincere,
He acted well from year to year;
An upright servant, well approved,
Respected, honour'd, and beloved.

Come present comforts as they will,
Old habits cling around us still;
And William often sigh'd to share
His father's toil in open air:
To roam the fields at early morn,
To plough the ground, and reap the
        corn;
And he in leisure hours, of late,
Had thought upon the marriage state.
Fanny, a giddy thoughtless flirt,
Too fond of finery and dirt,
Since first she came to Broughton
        Hall
Had set her cap at William Ball.
But William look'd another way;
He clearly saw in Esther May,

A humble, thoughtful, pious mind,
To active industry inclined ;
And fancied that with such a wife
How pleasantly would pass his life,
In some neat cottage!—'twas a
  thought
That often dreams of pleasure
  brought.
When love is pure, and free from art,
It softens and refines the heart :
Our varied passions onward press ;
And promise lasting happiness,
But love is still, 'mid all the rest,
The brightest glow that warms the
  breast.
'Tis only when by folly led
It brings a curse upon our head ;
For then, the fatal flame beware !
Come sin and sorrow and despair.

A humble home at Dunlop Hill
Was William's favourite project still.
The more he saw of Esther May,
The more he liked her day by day.
How sweet, in some neat white-
  wash'd cot,
To share with her his humble lot!
To see her happy, as his wife,
And lead a calm, religious life !
In such a quiet, blest retreat,
His happiness would be complete.
When hope turns painter to the heart,
How fair is life in every part !
She bids its future hours arise,
And decks its scenes with rainbow
  dyes.
But soon experience takes his stand ;
Snatches the pencil from her hand ;
Softens the gaudy colours down,
And spreads a shade of sober brown.

This life, with all the bliss it bears,
Must still remain a life of cares.
But grace can quench its trial fires,
Can turn its very thorns and briars
To blessings, and in love bestow
A heavenly balm for earthly woe.
Where'er the Saviour's love is shed,
It lifts the downcast heart and head,
Bids hope and joy and glory rise
To lure the spirit to the skies.
'Twas William's practice in his place,
To spread before the throne of grace

His hopes, his fears, his plans, his all,
That heavenly light around might fall,
To guide, in doubtful paths below,
His feet the way that they should go ;
And well it were if one and all
Would do the same as William Ball.
When William Ball, without display,
Had won the heart of Esther May,
His joy could hardly be exprest,
A grateful feeling fill'd his breast ;
And many a prayer he pour'd on high,
That God their hearts would sanctify
And help them to set forth his praise
In all their thoughts, their words, and
  ways,
As worshippers at Jesus' throne,
And clinging to his cross alone.

When William Ball to Roger ran
To tell him of his marriage plan,
He found him near the aged oak.
The good man smiled, and thus he
  spoke :—
" Why, Will," said he with open eyes,
" You take me rather by surprise ;
" Yet I should hardly act the man,
" To throw cold water on your plan,
" For I have found a prudent wife
" The greatest comfort of my life :
" But hungry mouths, Will, must be
  fed ;
" E'en love requires a loaf of bread,
" Or angry words and rough debate
" Will quickly turn it into hate.
" Before you take a wife, my lad,
" A little money must be had,
" To make secure the means to live.
" Now, money I have none to give,
" And you, I know, in worldly pelf,
" Are not much richer than myself.
" Your poor relations, one and all,
" Can speak in praise of William Ball.
" On acts of kindness always bent,
" They knew the way your wages went.
" Suppose you wait awhile, and see
" How things will turn : 'tween you
  and me
" A year may make, as things befall,
" A world of difference in us all."
Whene'er it thwarts our wayward will,
The best advice is painful still.
As William from the cottage went,
He felt a sort of discontent

Steal o'er his mind : to be debarr'd
From all his fairy dreams was hard.
"The Squire," thought he, the hope
    was bright,
"May see things in a different light.
"He will not, cannot be unkind ;
"At all events, I'll speak my mind."
With hasty feet he sought the
    Squire,
And quickly told his fond desire ;
And hemm'd, and blush'd, and made
    a stand,
And smooth'd his hat crown with his
    hand.

The Squire was much inclined to
    joke,
And laugh'd outright as thus he
    spoke :—
"No! no! Will Ball, I won't con-
    sent ;
"Why can't you stop with me con-
    tent ?
"I'll raise your wages ; Esther too
"Shall have a pound beyond her due,
"And that will please her, never
    fear ;
"So put it off another year.
"These early marriages may prove
"Right pleasant things to folks in
    love ;
"But when the cares of want arise,
"Love quickly through the window
    flies.
"Take my advice, you'll find it best,
"And put it off twelve months, at
    least."

Alas! the Squire, who spoke so free,
Lived not that twelvemonth's end to
    see ;
Before the year had run its round,
His dust was mouldering in the
    ground.
His mind to holy things was led
By William's piety, that shed

A grateful influence over all
The neighbourhood of Broughton
    Hall.
Severe affliction, sanctified,
Brought low his erring heart of
    pride ;
And, conscious of his coming end,
He sought and found the sinner's
    Friend.
Though grace its cordial gifts supply,
'Tis yet a solemn thing to die ;
And William quicker drew his breath,
In pondering o'er the bed of death.

The funeral over, William Ball
Soon bade farewell to Broughton Hall.
The Squire had left him in his will
That pleasant cot at Dunlop Hill ;
Where now he leads a tranquil life
With Esther May, his valued wife.
There have been seasons sad, 'tis true
But they were very, very few,
When William's temper, quick and
    proud,
Broke out in passions strong and
    loud :
But Esther, with a temper meek,
Knew how to bear and when to speak ;
His anger met with words of balm,
And soon the storm became a calm.

They live, with reputation fair,
A prudent, useful, pious pair ;
In times of joy and sorrow found
A blessing to their neighbours round.
And often, in affection free,
They sit beneath the spreading tree
At Roger's cot : the aged pair
Are always pleased to meet them
    there ;
For then they love the road to trace
That God has led them by his grace,
And join their voices clear to raise
A hymn in their Redeemer's praise,
Through whose atoning sacrifice
They hope to heaven above to rise.

THE RELIGIOUS TRACT SOCIETY ;
56, PATERNOSTER ROW, AND 164, PICCADILLY.

THE

COTTAGE MAID;

or,

HARRIET BELL.

———

PART I.—HER EARLY LIFE—HER CONDUCT IN SERVICE.
PART II.—HER HAPPY MARRIAGE.

LONDON:

THE RELIGIOUS TRACT SOCIETY;
56, PATERNOSTER ROW; AND 164, PICCADILLY.

c. 1804.

THE

COTTAGE MAID.

PART I.

HER EARLY LIFE.—HER CONDUCT IN SERVICE.

AND have you in your rambles seen,
A cottage on some village green,
The whitewash'd walls and trellis'd
    door,
With rose and jessamine hung o'er?
In such a home once used to dwell
The village maiden, Harriet Bell.
It must be fifty years or more,
Since first I trod that cottage floor,
Yet in my wanderings around,
So neat a spot I ne'er have found.

And Harriet Bell had cause to raise
Her heart in thankfulness and praise,
For she was bless'd with parents kind,
Who carefully watch'd o'er her mind.
At five years old she learned to spell,
And knew her catechism well;
Could sew and knit a little too,
And many other things could do.
Before she laid her down in bed
Her evening prayer was duly said;
And when she woke with morning
    light,
Her praise arose for her good night.
Industrious, thoughtful, modest, kind,
How few such children do we find!

Yet there were times when Harriet
    found
Much evil in her heart abound;
When pride and angry passions swell'd
Her little breast, and she rebell'd
Against the God of truth and grace;
Ah! then her sorrows flow'd apace,
Her tender mind was full of grief,
And she could never find relief

Till she to Heaven had poured her
    prayer,
And sought for Christ's forgiveness
    there;
Whose precious blood, and that alone,
Can for our guilty souls atone.

Oh, what a privilege to go
To God himself in time of wo!
To God himself, through Christ, and
    prove
His wisdom, faithfulness, and love!
Among my mercies let me place
That gift of gifts, a throne of grace;
There let me seek, and find supplies
Of grace to cleanse, and make me wise

Two miles was Harriet Bell from
    school,
But it had ever been her rule,
Summer and winter, rain or fair,
To be the first, the foremost there,
Her lessons learnt the night before,
She wak'd at morn and conn'd them
    o'er;
And all who knowledge have in view
This practice wisely should pursue.

Harriet, at morning's earliest ray,
Was thankful for another day,
And praising God for sweet repose,
Light hearted from her knees arose.
She soon despatched her milk and
    bread;
"Good morrow," to her parents said;
Then gaily tripp'd along the green;
Nor ever loitering was seen

Like girls and boys who vainly play,
And idle all their time away.
Attentive, tractable, she grew
In knowledge and in virtue too.
As years roll'd on they left no trace
Of evil passions on her face.
In usefulness and deeds of love
She liv'd, and fix'd her heart above.
Esteem'd by all who knew her well,
And much belov'd was Harriet Bell.

But now the time was drawing nigh,
When she must quit, with tear and
  sigh,
The pretty cottage on the green,
And leave that dear, that quiet scene,
Of childhood's joys, of childhood's
  cares,
And enter on a world of snares.

A lady living far remote,
A letter to a neighbour wrote,
Said that a friend had spoken well
Of the young maiden, Harriet Bell;
And she was willing to engage
The granddaughter of Hannah Page,
As nursemaid to Miss Clara Nind,
Who had for several years been blind.
When Harriet saw her way was clear,
She parted from her parents dear,
And went to service with a mind
Contented, cheerful, and resign'd.

It is a trying time, I know,
When servants first to service go;
And every one has need of grace
To aid her entering on her place.
But let such servants look on high,
And trust in Christ's sufficiency ;
And they shall find his grace and
  power
Support and guide them every hour.
This Harriet knew, and look'd above,
For strength that she might ever prove,
In every thought, and deed, and word,
A faithful servant of the Lord.

With tender care, and manners kind,
She waited on Miss Clara Nind ;
Most faithfully performed her part
And won poor little Clara's heart.
In summer oft they rambled wide,
And, seated on the green hill side,

Clara would learn so quick and well,
To say her hymns to Harriet Bell ;
And Harriet dearly lov'd the child,
And all her little cares beguil'd ;
Tried much to raise her thoughts
  above,
And told her of a Saviour's love.
And He who hears when infants raise
Their lisping strains of prayer and
  praise,
Heard Clara's voice, and gave her
  grace,
And made her heart his dwelling place.
But soon it pleas'd a God of love
To take this happy child above,
And Harriet Bell durst not repine ;
She knew the darling child would
  shine
Like a bright star in heaven's high
  sphere,
And reign with Christ for ever there.

And now she quitted, with regret,
A house where she had ever met
With kindness, and been valued long
By every inmate, old and young.
The servant who is faithful found,
Will be respected all around ;
But she, who quits in sad disgrace,
How shall she get another place ?

Poor Harriet rais'd her voice in
  prayer,
That God again would guide her where
She might be happy, useful found,
And ever in his grace abound.
As under laundry-maid she next
Engag'd herself, but was perplex'd
To find, down in the servants' hall,
The giddy maiden, Sarah Wall.
Yet honest, active, faithful, kind,
Harriet still kept her peace of mind,
While thoughtless Sarah, in disgrace,
Soon lost, by conduct bad, her place.

At first she felt with much concern,
That she had every thing to learn;
But, not discourag'd, still she stay'd,
Till she was upper-laundry-maid.

Myton was then a sweet abode,
Half a mile distant from the road.

Woods, gardens, pleasure grounds were
there
Laid out with nicest taste and care ;
And crowds on summer days were seen
Rambling about on Myton green,
Or calmly sitting by the side
Of the clear brook at eventide.

Now Harriet had some virtues rare
Not many in her station share ;
Wherever she might chance to dwell
She never needlessly would tell
Of faults and failings, which she found
Did, more or less, in all abound.
And she had ever from her youth
Adher'd most strictly to the truth.
Those who had known her long and
well
Could never of a falsehood tell.
She fearful was of every sin ;
She would not dare to steal a pin ;
And oft the truth repeated o'er,
" A trifling theft may lead to more."
In sickness she was prompt and kind,
And show'd great tenderness of mind.

It was the wish of Harriet Bell
In love and peace with all to dwell.
From morn to night she was employ'd ;
And sadly was her mind annoy'd
When fellow servants, pert and vain,
Would of their place and work com-
plain.
She oft assur'd them, as a friend,
Repining would to evil tend ;
And though her words reach'd not
their heart,
She knew that she had done her part :
She felt contented, and at rest,
And happiness reign'd in her breast.

Amidst the cares and mingled strife
Of every kind that trouble life,
One thing is sure—the pious mind
In every state will comfort find :
And faith in Jesus Christ imparts
An inward peace to contrite hearts.

Tho years roll'd on—still Harriet
stay'd
At Myton Hall as laundry-maid ;
For she believ'd it a disgrace
To change about from place to place.

She would not for a trifle part,
And knew so much of her own heart,
That she ne'er vainly sought to find
Perfection in another's mind.

There is no situation free
From trouble and anxiety ;
Nor should we suffer fancies vain
To give unnecessary pain.
At first her wages were but small,
But yet, she never spent them all ;
No vain desires had she to feed,
But part laid by for time of need.
At length the maiden Harriet Bell
Of one and twenty pounds could tell,
Which she had well contriv'd to spare,
And put by with prudential care :
The sum, secure from sinful waste,
Within a savings'-bank was placed,
While, every year, the interest due
Was added to the money too.
Thus, trusting in her Saviour's grace,
She went on prospering in her place.

When she a holiday could share,
It was not at a village fair ;
And Harriet Bell had never been
At theatres or dances seen.
When she had leave, she lov'd to
spend
A pleasant evening with a friend ;
But never gossiping was known ;
She said her time was not her own.
Neither through thoughtlessness nor
haste
Would she a trifle ever waste.
Good-natured, steady, and serene,
And seldom in a bustle seen,
Each thing when us'd she put away,
And thus avoided much delay.
Some girls may search the house
around,
Before a proper brush be found,
But Harriet, with becoming grace,
Put every thing in its own place.
It was her constant aim and care,
To be the tidiest maiden there.
Then, rising at the morning's prime,
She ne'er complain'd of want of time,
But, sometimes, half a day could
spare,
To keep her clothes in good repair.

PART II.

HER HAPPY MARRIAGE.

ABOUT this time the coachman made
An offer to the cottage maid,
But she would not accept his hand,
Though he possess'd a house and land,
Because he ridicul'd as nought
The high salvation Christ has wrought.
He often urg'd his suit in vain;
Then treated Harriet with disdain;
Call'd her a hypocrite, and prude,
And teas'd her with his conduct rude.
But she was not to be dismay'd,
Well knowing where to look for aid.

If o'er this little simple book,
A servant girl should chance to look,
Who means, with some respected
   mate,
To enter on the marriage state,
Let her thus put her questions free
Of him who would her husband be :—
Is he a man whose deed and word
Would lead my heart to fear the
   Lord ?

Would he hold on the heavenly race
And join me at the throne of grace ?
When all our earthly paths are trod,
Might we expect to dwell with God ?
These questions let her put, and pray
For grace to guide her on her way.

Simply and modestly array'd
Was the young lively cottage maid.
Harriet would neat and clean appear
But did not dress above her sphere.
She never studied to be fine,
Nor wish'd in gaudy gowns to shine,
And when it was her Sunday out,
Instead of wandering about,
She with a friend in reverence trod
That bless'd resort, the house of God.
And while she rais'd her heart on
   high,
She found her God, her Saviour
   nigh,
With rich supplies of grace to stay,
Her soul through every coming day.

And train'd their children, three were
    given,
With unremitting care for heaven.
Thus, bless'd on every hand around,
Old age this happy couple found:
They liv'd in faith, in hope, and love,
And now have join'd the bless'd above.

If, reader, thou hast ponder'd well
This little tale of Harriet Bell,
And marked the end it has in view,
Be wise, and make it useful too.
Whene'er we take a book in hand,
And try its sense to understand,
'Tis well to read with temper meek,
And wisdom more than pleasure seek;
For pleasure is, at best, a spark
That fades, and leaves us in the dark;
But wisdom is a steady star,
That throws its milder beams afar,
And sheds on earth a grateful ray,
To light us on our heavenly way.

I tell no marvellous tale to bind
An idle fiction on thy mind;
To raise thy wonder, and employ
Thy heart with momentary joy;
But, rather, common life display,
And things which happen every day.
Thou, in thy youth, like Harriet Bell,
Hast learn'd at school to read and
    spell,
And soon, on upright ways intent
Perhaps to service will be sent.

Take courage, then, nor be dismay'd,
But pray in faith, as Harriet pray'd,
That God, for Jesus' sake would bind
His law and love upon thy mind, ·
And guide and guard thee by his
    power,
Through every day, and every hour.
Without his favour, thou wilt be
Unstable as the restless sea;
But with his grace within thy soul,
Thy days and nights will tranquil roll.
While countless cares and troubles fall
On thoughtless girls, like Sarah Wall,
A thousand peaceful pleasures dwell
With servants such as Harriet Bell.
With all thy soul right onward press,
And seek the Lord our righteousness;
For those who early seek his face
Shall find him, and partake his grace.
And Jesus Christ, who died to save,
Shall give them hope beyond the grave
His death their life, his pleas above
The source and succour of their love;
While treading with a steady pace
The paths of holiness and peace.

If thou art thoughtless, proud, and
    still
Determin'd on thy wayward will,
The counsel that I give will be,
Alas! of little use to thee;
But if discreet, and meek, and wise,
Thy humbled heart will ne'er despise
The simple story, here display'd,
Of Harriet Bell, the Cottage Maid.

LONDON: THE RELIGIOUS TRACT SOCIETY; 56, PATERNOSTER ROW.
PRICE ONE PENNY.

www.ingramcontent.com/pod-product-compliance
Lightning Source LLC
Chambersburg PA
CBHW030619270326
41927CB00007B/1244